CITIZENS CONGRESS

COMMON SENSE FOR THE TWENTY FIRST CENTURY

CITIZENS CONGRESS

Common Sense for the Twenty First Century

By

Dan Barnett

Citizens Congress

Copyright © 2018

By

Dan Barnett

ISBN – 9781724112767

Library of Congress application has been submitted.

Cover design and photos by Dan Barnett

Written by Dan Barnett, who is solely responsible for its contents. Any errors are unintentional but are the responsibility of the author.

DEDICATION

To the people who inspired not only this writing, but the idea for Citizens Congress itself.

When I was 27 I quit my job with the largest company in the world to have an adventure. Selling home and possessions, I went on the road with money in the bank and a backpack on my shoulders. I would hitchhike for the next three years, except for the coldest months, crisscrossing North America several times and visiting 49 of our 50 states. I camped most nights and discovered the incredible natural beauty of our National Parks and Forests. At times I was in wilderness far from humans, but at home with the trees and mountains. We live in an incredibly beautiful country.

However, what impressed me even more were the people. Hitchhiking was easy in the late seventies. I could go coast to coast in a few days. During those years I had thousands of rides. Hitching is an intimate experience. People told me their life stories, what they loved, and where they had been. The offered me food and money (which I refused) thinking because of my choice of travel I might be in need. Often drivers would go far out of their way to drop me at my destination. More than a few offered their home for the night. I remain to this day overwhelmed at the level of human kindness I experienced during those years. I have found that most people are good, kind, and decent.

Also in my twenties, I was called for jury duty and chosen for a murder trial. I still remember feeling the weight of responsibility as I sat in the jury box. I could feel it in my fellow jurors as well. We listened carefully. We examined and weighed the evidence. We voted our conscience while dutifully following the law.

Like hitchhiking, jury duty is still a vivid memory. These two experiences left me with an abiding faith in my fellow man. I went on to work as a telephone technician. That took me into thousands of homes, from the wealthiest to the most impoverished. It only reinforced my belief that people are overwhelmingly good. That is why I can propose a Citizens Congress. It is why I can believe that if we take 1000 people, chosen at random from the pool of registered voters, and seat them in Congress, that they will listen carefully, examine and weigh the evidence, vote their conscience, and do the right thing. I dedicate this writing and Citizens Congress to you, the American people.

FOREWORD

"If liberty and equality, as is thought by some, are chiefly to be found in democracy, they will be best attained when all persons alike share in government to the utmost."

Aristotle

When I first read this quote, I realized it was not necessary to ask someone to write a foreword to this book. They already had. Aristotle lived more than 2300 years ago and yet his words embody the spirit of Citizens Congress with more eloquence than I possess. Let us see what some of the most respected minds in history have written about democracy.

"I know no safe depositary of the ultimate powers of the society but the people themselves; and if we think them not enlightened enough to exercise their control with a wholesome discretion, the remedy is not to take it from them, but to inform their discretion by education."

Thomas Jefferson

"Real liberty is neither found in despotism or the extremes of democracy, but in moderate governments."

Alexander Hamilton

"Democracy, pure democracy, has at least its foundation in a generous theory of human rights. It is founded on the natural equality of mankind."

John Quincy Adams

"The strength of the Constitution lies entirely in the determination of each citizen to defend it. Only if every single citizen feels duty bound to do

his share in this defense are the constitutional rights secure."

Albert Einstein

"Anywhere, anytime ordinary people are given the chance to choose, the choice is the same: freedom, not tyranny; democracy, not dictatorship; the rule of law, not the rule of the secret police."

Tony Blair

"Our safety, our liberty, depends upon preserving the Constitution of the United States as our fathers made it inviolate. The people of the United States are the rightful masters of both Congress and the courts, not to overthrow the Constitution, but to overthrow the men who pervert the Constitution."

Abraham Lincoln

*"We hold these truths to be self-evident, that all men are created equal, that they are endowed by their Creator with certain unalienable Rights that among these are Life, Liberty and the pursuit of Happiness. — That to secure these rights, Governments are instituted among Men, **deriving their just powers from the consent of the governed, — That whenever any Form of Government becomes destructive of these ends, it is the Right of the People to alter or to abolish it,** and to institute new Government, laying its foundation on such principles and organizing its powers in such form, as to them shall seem most likely to effect their Safety and Happiness."*

Declaration of Independence.

"Prudence, indeed, will dictate that Governments long established should not be changed for light and transient causes; and accordingly all experience hath shewn that mankind are more disposed to suffer, while evils are sufferable than to right themselves by abolishing the forms to which they are accustomed. But when a long train of abuses and usurpations, pursuing invariably the same Object evinces a design to

reduce them under absolute Despotism, it is their right, it is their duty, to throw off such Government, and to provide new Guards for their future security."

Declaration of Independence

"Concentrated power has always been the enemy of liberty. Democracy is worth dying for, because it's the most deeply honorable form of government ever devised by man."

Ronald Reagan

"The liberty of a democracy is not safe if the people tolerated the growth of private power to a point where it becomes stronger than the democratic state itself. That in its essence is fascism: ownership of government by an individual, by a group, or any controlling private power."

Franklin D. Roosevelt

"Democracy is a device that insures we shall be governed no better than we deserve."

George Bernard Shaw

"I would rather be governed by the first 2000 people in the Manhattan phone book than the entire faculty of Harvard."

William F. Buckley Jr.

"It is the people who control the Government, not the Government the people."

Winston S. Churchill

"that this nation, under God, shall have a new birth of freedom-and that government of the people, by the people, for the people shall not perish from the earth."

Abraham Lincoln

CONTENTS

DEDICATION   9

FOREWORD   13

CITIZENS CONGRESS   25

WHY DO WE NEED THIS   29
AMENDMENT?

WHY IS IT SO IMPORTANT?   31

CAN WE END LEGALIZED   35
CORRUPTION?

ISN'T IT HARD TO PASS A   37
CONSTITUTIONAL AMENDMENT?

WHY 1000 PEOPLE? ISN'T THAT JUST 41
AN ARBITRARY NUMBER?

WHY IS THIS BETTER THAN AN   43
ELECTED GOVERNMENT?

ONE PERSON/ONE VOTE   47

HISTORY

BUT WHAT ABOUT NOW?

GERRYMANDERING

ELECTORAL COLLEGE

LOBBYISTS

VOTING RIGHTS OF FELONS

THE DISENFRANCHISED   57

BY GENDER

BY AGE

BY INCOME

BY OCCUPATION

BY PARTY AFFILIATION

WILL CITIZENS BE REQUIRED   69
TO SERVE?

IS THE GENERAL PUBLIC QUALIFIED TO SERVE? — 71

OTHER ISSUES: — 76

ALTERNATES

TYRANNY OF THE MINORITY

PRIMARY DUTIES OF THE THREE BRANCHES — 80

LEGISLATIVE (CONGRESS)

EXECUTIVE (PRESIDENT)

JUDICIAL (SUPREME COURT AND

LOWER COURTS)

THE PROBLEMS WITH THE CONGRESS WE HAVE — 85

PARTISANSHIP

CHECKS AND BALANCES

WHAT ABOUT THE PRESIDENCY?

FUNDRAISING

PLATA O PLOMO---SILVER OR LEAD

LOBBYISTS

A HOUSE DIVIDED   101

FREQUENTLY ASKED QUESTIONS   105

PROPOSED 27TH AMENDMENT TO   115
THE CONSTITUTION OF THE UNITED
STATES OF AMERICA

CITIZENS CONGRESS INC.   125

CONTACT INFORMATION   128

ABOUT THE AUTHOR   129

EPILOGUE   132

CITIZENS CONGRESS

Common Sense for the Twenty First Century

The purpose of Citizens Congress is to write, propose, and promote, the passage of an amendment to the Constitution redefining the structure of the Congress of the United States. This can only be done by the amendment process because it is the Constitution that establishes and defines Congress. Citizens Congress Inc. is a non-partisan, grass roots, Not-for-Profit Corporation founded to achieve those goals.

Included is a first draft of the Amendment to introduce the basic concepts. It is expected to undergo a thorough examination by academics, experts in Constitutional Law, and especially the three hundred and twenty five million Americans for whom the Constitution offers structure to their government and protection of their rights. It will be revised as necessary to protect against unintended consequences, and to insure it achieves its goals. It will then be offered to the public for their approval. If the people decide the Amendment is in the best interest of maintaining a just and free society, it will be their duty to petition the Government for its passage.

As the Amendment is of necessity lengthy, its most important points will be summarized here, and then further explained. The first draft of the Amendment will appear in the final pages.

The heart of the Citizens Congress proposal is to replace the 435 elected members of the House of Representatives with a body of 1000 members selected at random by lottery from the pool of registered voters who are United States Citizens. These Representatives will be apportioned to each State according to population.

The Senate would remain the same, with the exception that the Senate would send legislation to the House for approval but the House of Representatives could send legislation directly to the President without Senate approval. Senate elections would also be publicly funded to eliminate the undue influence of moneyed interests.

As elections would be eliminated in the House and publicly funded in the Senate, lobbyists would be prohibited from providing anything of monetary value to any member of Congress under penalty of imprisonment.

Paid lobbyists would be prohibited from approaching any member of Congress to influence their vote or pass any information to them, unless that communication was provided in an open forum with full access to the public. If Congress was considering legislation that affected industries, large groups of people, etc. they could invite interested parties to testify under oath. Anyone choosing to lie or present false data to Congress would face perjury charges and time in prison.

The other significant change would lower the age to serve in the House of Representatives to match the age of military service, eighteen years.

The result, if the Citizens Congress Amendment were to become law, would be seating the full spectrum of American Citizens in the House of Representatives. Every demographic, by income, gender, race, occupation, political affiliation, and countless other parameters would receive their fair proportion in representation in the House of Representatives.   The Senate also would be enhanced by freeing every Senator, from the need to beg wealthy donors for money, and enabling individual Senators or groups of Senators to directly propose legislation to the House with or without party approval and to vote their conscience on every issue.

WHY DO WE NEED THIS AMENDMENT?

Our Congress has drifted far from our founders intent and quite distant from acting in the best interest of the American people. This failure is reflected in Congress's approval rating which was 16% as of September 2017. This low opinion is held by citizens of both parties, and independents as well.

Despite the low approval rating, over 90% of incumbents are reelected. Voters, even though they know Congress is broken, see no alternative to the system we have and are largely resigned to the status quo. Citizens Congress offers a real change that would replace our failed Congress with a cross section of American voters.

"I know no safe depositary of the ultimate powers of the society but the people themselves; and if we think them not enlightened enough to exercise their control with a wholesome discretion, the remedy is not to take it from them, but to inform their discretion by education. This is the true corrective of abuses of constitutional power."

Thomas Jefferson

Our founders risked their lives and fortunes to escape the injustice found under British rule. They saw the folly of government far removed from control of the governed. *"WE THE PEOPLE",* the first three words of the Constitution, embody the spirit of the whole document. They did not hazard their very lives to trade one tyranny for another. It is "We the People" that must determine our own destiny. Citizens Congress fixes the problem of not having a truly representative government by putting a cross section of American voters firmly in charge of our government.

WHY IS IT SO IMPORTANT?

Congress, at the federal level, passes all the laws that we live under. They collect all the taxes and spend all the money. They have the sole power to declare war on other nations. They decide how much to regulate our industries and, within the boundaries of the Constitution, what freedoms we may enjoy. They approve appointments for life to the Supreme Court. Every amendment to the Constitution has passed through Congress. However, Congress has ceased to be the voice of the people for two reasons. Even though they were chosen to represent their districts and states, and the people therein, they are more beholding to their parties and their donors. Even though 42 percent of voters are registered as independents, there are only two independents in Congress.

Party membership is essential to getting elected and reelected. Without party support, it is almost impossible. That support comes at a price. The pressure to vote along party lines is tremendous. We would want our representative to vote for what is good for our district, our state, and our country. However, if they do not vote with their party they may find themselves without support for the next election. They also need enormous amounts of money for reelection. That means spending 20 to 30 hours a week (CBS 60 Minutes estimate) calling wealthy individuals and corporate donors asking for money. They also spend many hours with lobbyists listening to what their donors want in return for millions in campaign donations. That money comes at a price. The donors expect a return on their investment and are watching every vote. This leaves us with Congressmen who are more concerned about their party and their donors than the people who hired them to do the job. Citizens Congress removes all the money from Congressional politics by removing elections in the House of Representatives and publicly funding elections in the Senate. It takes away the stranglehold the parties have over their members and the open bribery of the lobbyists. In short, it fixes what is wrong with Congress.

"No man's life, liberty, or property is safe while the legislature is in session."

Gideon J. Tucker

CAN WE END LEGALIZED CORRUPTION?

With our current system our Congressman need to raise millions of dollars to win re-election. House members need an average of $1.6 million every two years to run. Senate campaigns top $10 million. More than 12,000 lobbyists spend over $3 billion per year to influence Congress. This money comes mostly from extremely wealthy individuals and corporations. These are businesspersons. They are not patriots seeking to help their country. They are expecting Return on Investment. It is legal, for instance, for lobbyists working for the big banks, to offer millions in donations to the head of the committee charged with oversight of the banking industry. They can then write legislation they want and hand it to their Congressman. When he retires, he can go to work for the very industry that paid him off and collect a million dollar salary as a "Consultant", or become a lobbyist himself. No laws have been broken. Corruption has been made legal. Citizens Congress would end it.

The House would have no elections. The Senate elections would be fully publicly funded with no private contributions allowed. Lobbyists would be prevented from contacting any Congressman except through public channels. They would have to be invited to speak to Congress in a public forum and under oath. Backroom deals would end. Passage of unscrupulous legislation at 3 a.m. while the public sleeps would end. We can end corruption and have the government we deserve if we have the will to do it.

ISN'T IT HARD TO PASS A CONSTITUTIONAL AMENDMENT?

Yes, it can be very hard. Some are never passed. The Equal Rights Amendment was approved by Congress and 35 states but has not reached the 38 states needed to become law. However, the 26th Amendment was ratified in just three months and eight days in 1971 lowering the voting age from 21 to 18. An amendment must clearly reflect the will of the people. It must be proposed by a two thirds majority of both houses of Congress or by two thirds of the state legislatures convening a Constitutional Convention. After passing this test, it must be approved by three quarters of the state legislatures. Passage would require tremendous public pressure on our Federal and State governments to change a system that is working very well for them but not so well for the rest of us. Citizens Congress will be difficult to achieve, but it was hard to defeat the strongest army and navy in the world to win our freedom from English rule. It was hard to survive the Great Depression. It was hard to fight two World Wars to maintain our freedom. We do hard things. America was made for this!

The actual wording from Article V of the Constitution is: *"The Congress, whenever two thirds of both Houses shall deem it necessary, shall propose Amendments to this Constitution, or, on the Application of the Legislatures of two thirds of the several States, shall call a Convention for proposing Amendments, which, in either Case, shall be valid to all Intents and Purposes, as part of this Constitution, when ratified by the Legislatures of three fourths of the several States, or by Conventions in three fourths thereof."*

To accomplish this we need the votes of two thirds of either the U.S. Congress or the state legislatures. Then we need ratification by three quarters of the state legislatures. This can be accomplished by only electing candidates that pledge to vote in favor of Citizens Congress. The longest term an American politician serves is six years. If we want a government *of and for the people*, we can replace every politician in our country in only six years. We the People are granted this right by the very Constitution we seek to amend. Thank you, Founding Fathers, for your wisdom and foresight.

"I should sooner live in a society governed by the first two thousand names in the Boston telephone directory than in a society governed by the two thousand faculty members of Harvard University"

William F. Buckley Jr.

WHY 1000 PEOPLE? ISN'T THAT JUST AN ARBITRARY NUMBER?

Yes, the 435 members we have now is an arbitrary number, chosen when we had a much smaller population, and 1000 is also arbitrary. However, it was not chosen by accident. Mathematicians assure us that a poll using just 1000 people will be within 3 percentage points of being as accurate as if we polled every person in the country. Just as a chef needs only a spoonful of sauce to know if his dish is spiced correctly, we do not need to poll every American. But the chef must first stir the pot well. Likewise, we must not skew the poll by accidentally, or deliberately obscuring the meaning of the question, or hand picking those whom we query. We must take a truly random sampling to have an honest poll, and we must use a truly random method to insure every American Citizen that is registered to vote has an equal chance to serve in Congress.

WHY IS THIS BETTER THAN AN ELECTED GOVERNMENT?

The problem with the representative government we have now is simply that it is not representative. It differs in many significant ways. The Congress we have now looks very little like America. With over 50% millionaires, they are out of touch with the realities of working people. In one twelve year period Congress voted themselves 3 pay raises totaling over 20%. During that same period, they did not raise the Federal Minimum Pay Rate by one penny. It demonstrates how little they care about the problems of working Americans. A Citizens

Congress would be in touch with working class people because the majority of them would be working class people. Millionaires tend to write laws that are good for millionaires. It is easy to see how very well millionaires and billionaires are doing while working people see their wages and quality of life stagnate. Information released by Pew Research in August of 2018 says real wages (adjusted for inflation) have been stagnant for American workers for 40 years. Worker productivity has grown immensely during that time, but the profits have gone to richest individuals and corporations. Again, Pew tells us in a January 2017 study that the minimum wage peaked in buying power in 1968 and was worth about 20% less in 2016. We pay a heavy price for not taking care of the working poor. We have too many working people who cannot afford the basics of life. In some cases, we, the taxpayers, are partially supporting full time workers when their employers could be paying a living wage. It is likely that a Congress, which included a large proportion of working people, would do what our wealthy Congressmen have refused to do. They would pass a fair, reasonable minimum wage law. This is just one of many issues that demonstrates how out of touch Congress is with the population at large. On many topics, the public has 70% or greater agreement but Congress makes a different choice. It is time to let the people decide their own fate. Only Citizens Congress achieves that. Passing the Constitutional Amendment needed will be challenging but we have done harder things than this. It depends on our ability to see that our common needs outweigh our differences, and that we are stronger together than separately. Congress is broken. We can fix this.

"We must vote for hope, vote for life, vote for a brighter future for all of our loved ones."

Ed Markey

ONE PERSON/ONE VOTE

HISTORY:

One person/one vote seems to be a basic concept. It is simple and fair. It gives every Citizen an equal voice in government. It was not however, what we started with, or what we have now.

Some of the founders thought the vote should be weighted so that those with more money or land should have more votes. In the end the Constitution, when signed in 1789, left voting rights up to the states. Generally, they decided that everyone could vote, as long as they were white, male, and owned land or paid taxes. That was about 6% of the population.

A few states granted free black men the vote, and later rescinded that right. The presidential election of 1928 marks the first time that the vast majority of white males, including those who owned no land, could vote. It took the 14th Amendment to the Constitution to grant voting rights to all male persons born or naturalized in the United States.

Apparently "all" was not clear enough to some of the states. Two years later we passed the 15th Amendment to clarify that states could not deny the right to vote on grounds of "race, color, or previous condition of servitude". The southern states went right to work on poll taxes, literacy tests, and other restrictions to prevent black males from voting.

In 1920, after a bitter struggle, the other half of our Citizens won the right to vote. Women had been ridiculed, beaten, jailed, and sent to insane asylums in the process. That was the Nineteenth Amendment to the Constitution.

Yes, Constitutional Amendments can happen, but we need to work for it, and sometimes fight for it.

In 1961 the Twenty Third Amendment granted voting rights to residents of Washington D.C.. Three years later, the Twenty Fourth Amendment finally prohibited the poll tax. States could no longer force people to pay for the privilege of voting in Federal elections. Of course, the poll tax was only designed to keep the "wrong people" from voting.

It took the draft and the Viet Nam war to end the next major injustice in voting rights. The average age of front line combat soldiers in that war was 19 years old. No one under the age of 21 was allowed to vote for the President or Congress that sent them to war. On March 23rd 1971 the Twenty Sixth Amendment to the Constitution passed the House and Senate. Three months and eight days later it had been ratified by the three quarters of the states needed to make it law It was most rapid ratification of any Amendment ever. Citizens Congress would extend to 18 to 24 year old Citizens the right to serve in the House of Representatives and fully participate in our government.

With their taxes, their service, and sometimes their lives, they have earned the right.

Amendments to the Constitution can happen, and even happen quickly. They must be fair, and just, and have the support of the people.

BUT WHAT ABOUT NOW?

We have a long history of limiting the voting rights of the people. It has been a struggle to come this far. The battle is not yet won. There are still several ways in which we fall short of one person/one vote.

GERRYMANDERING:

The House of Representative's membership is apportioned to each state based on population. States are then divided into Congressional Districts. California has 53, Florida 27, and Delaware 1. Every ten years there is a census, and the districts are redrawn, based on the new census numbers. In many states the drawing of districts is controlled by the political party with the majority of legislators. When they rig the system in their favor it is called gerrymandering.

This has been done by both parties to very effectively gain unfair advantage in elections.

If party A and party B, for example, both have the same number of voters in a state but party A gets to draw the districts they will wind up with most of the seats in the House. Districts are drawn so that in most districts there is a majority of voters from party A. A state with a 30 districts might have 20 that are virtually certain to elect candidates from party A and 10 from party B. If you are a B voter living in an A weighted district no candidate you vote for is ever likely to be elected. **Instead of voters choosing their candidates, candidates are able to choose their voters.** A Citizens Congress could fix that by insuring districts are drawn based on simple geography by a disinterested entity under court supervision. In addition, without elections in the House, gerrymandering becomes useless. Every persons vote needs a fair chance to count. Citizens Congress would end gerrymandering in the U.S. Congress.

ELECTORAL COLLEGE:

The Electoral College is 538 people designated to elect the President. They are assigned to represent their states based on the number of Congressmen in their state. This creates an imbalance, as it includes Senators. Each state has two Senators, and the number of House members is based on population. This means an individual's vote in a small state like Nebraska with one Representative and two Senators carries more than three times the weight in the Electoral College than a voter in California with 53 Representatives.

Forty eight states are winner take all states. That means if fifty one percent of voters vote for candidate A, all of the states Electoral College votes go to candidate A. Citizens who voted for candidate B could have stayed home for all the difference it made. This leads to voter apathy and allows the possibility of a third problem.

Five times in our history Presidents have been elected by the Electoral College while losing the popular vote. We have the idea of one person/one vote, but the reality is much different.

Existing systems tend to favor whoever is in power. Neither party is likely to change this while they are in power or able to change it when not in power. A Citizens Congress serves a one year term, and each member is free from any constraints on their vote except their own thinking and conscience.

LOBBYISTS:

Lobbyists spend over 3 billion dollars a year on Capitol Hill. That is about 5.6 million dollars per Congressman. To win elections and reelections under the present system candidates need money and lots of it. It is perfectly legal for a lobbyist to walk into a Congressman's office with a check for hundreds of thousands of dollars in one hand and the legislation they want passed in the other. An investigation by Sixty Minutes reported that the average Congressman spends about twenty, to as many as thirty, hours a week on the phone begging rich donors for money. This is not only terrible for our democracy but also shameful for our elected officials to be reduced to being tele-marketers.

The First Amendment reads, *"Congress shall make no law respecting an establishment of religion, or prohibiting the free exercise thereof; or abridging the freedom of speech, or of the press; or the right of the people peaceably to assemble,* **and to petition the Government for a redress of grievances."**

The right to go to Congress and ask for what we want is of supreme importance to our Democracy. It is an equal right afforded all Citizens. It is also the law that allows lobbyists' to exist. It is not a problem for any individual, group, or representative of any group to address their Congressman and express their thoughts. It only becomes a problem when money is factored in. Citizens Congress can eliminate that problem. In the House, when we eliminate elections we eliminate campaign contributions. In the Senate, we publicly fund elections, again eliminating contributions. That gives everyone an equal voice when petitioning the government. Lobbyists would have only their ideas to offer to Congress.

VOTING RIGHTS OF FELONS:

In thirteen states, felons who have served their sentences are still not allowed to vote. Some are able to obtain a pardon, or go through a difficult and expensive process to regain this basic right. Nationwide about 6 million felons are barred from voting even after completing their incarceration, parole, and probation. We have a common principle that a person who breaks a law owes a debt to society. Those debts may be paid with fines, or, for more serious offences, prison. Part of that social contract however, is that once a person has paid their debt to society they have an opportunity to become a law abiding Citizen. In Florida, a person may have a felony record for writing a bad check, even without intent. Another may have spent a year or two in jail for drug possession. Nevertheless, even after thirty years of lawful, clean and sober living they can still be denied the right to vote.

At Citizens Congress, we believe every American should have an equal voice in government. Our position on every issue is "Put the people in power, and let the people decide."

Our Amendment would end gerrymandering, and take lobbyist money out of our elections. I believe it is likely that a Congress made up of the full spectrum of Citizens would act quickly to address the Electoral College and felons' voting rights. I believe America would finally achieve the goal of one person/one vote, an equal voice.

THE DISENFRANCHISED

BY GENDER:

Women hold just 19% of the seats in Congress. That is a record number, but far from their 51% representation in the population. They are 47% of the workforce. They pay taxes at the same rate as males.

Ninety-eight years after winning the right to vote, women are still nowhere near parity in Congress. How can we allow an 81% majority of men in Congress, and still say that we have a representative government?

Women have a different way of looking at many issues. It is not just that they deserve an equal voice in government. It is that we need to hear that voice. We need the balance that comes from hearing everyone's opinion.

Under Citizens Congress, women would hold the number of the seats they deserve. It has been almost 100 years since women won the right to vote, but they are still vastly underrepresented in Congress. If the Citizens Congress Constitutional Amendment passes, the next Congress would contain about 50% women.

BY AGE:

The current minimum age to serve in the House of Representatives is 25. For the Senate it is 30. The age to serve in the military however is 18. The vast majority of soldiers enter the military before they are 25. Countless thousands have given life and limb while still 18, 19, or 20. Until 1971, no one under the age of twenty-one even had the right to vote for those who sent them to war. This was corrected in 1971 when **we passed the 26th Amendment in just three months and eight days**, the fastest ratification in history.   Those who take on the greatest responsibility of citizenship must be not be denied full rights. As soldiers they can be called on to make some of the toughest decisions, often dealing with life and death matters. An eighteen or nineteen year old guard at a checkpoint in Afghanistan may have only seconds to decide if the woman in a burka approaching his post with a small child walking beside her is a suicide bomber or a mother in distress. If we can ask him to make that decision, he can decide whether to raise or lower a tax or make a trade deal with China.

Alexander Hamilton was in combat, fighting the British in the Revolutionary War, by the age of 18. When he was twenty George Washington made him a lieutenant colonel, and he became Washington's senior aide. Hamilton's friend, Lafayette, was born in the same year as Alexander. He was a major general by the age of 19. Lafayette was a significant ally, not only leading troops into victorious battles, but also lobbying the French government to increase aid to the Continental Army.

The average age of soldiers fighting on the front lines in the Vietnam War was 19.

Malala Yousafzai was just 17 when she won the Noble Peace Prize for her work on behalf of education for the world's girls.

At the age of 15, Louis Braille (who was blind) invented the Braille System of reading.

Steve Jobs was developing the first personal computer by the age of 19. Bill Gates founded Microsoft at the same age.

Modern air conditioning was invented by 20 year old Willis Carrier.

The list of incredible accomplishments by those under 25 would fill a book of its own.

Our young people also pay taxes at the same rate as the rest of us. *Taxation without representation* was the primary reason given for the American Revolution.

Sixty seven percent of Congressmen are over 55, while only twenty eight percent of our population is.

The average age of a Congress person is over 57 years, far older than the average adult population of our country. While it is true that young people lack experience, they bring a fresh exuberance to the table. They tend toward idealism and have fresh memories of high school and college courses in government and history that many of us who are older can scarcely recall. Those 18 to 24 year olds make up about 10% of our population. They have the right to serve, and add value to the blend of Citizen legislators. Their voices need to be heard. Citizens Congress could end this injustice.

BY INCOME:

"An imbalance between rich and poor is the oldest and most fatal ailment of all republics."

PLUTARCH

ANCIENT GREEK BIOGRAPHER

The median net worth of a member of Congress was $1.03 million in 2013. This is 18 times the worth of the average household. More than half of Congressmen are worth over a million dollars. Their base salary is $174,000.00 per year. The average wage earner receives $44,000.00 per year. Not one Congressman has to figure out how to live on the average wage, much less the $15,000.00 per year that minimum wage pays. A 20 year study by Stanford University based on wealth and income, revealed the top 10% got the legislation they approved of 70% of the time. The bottom 90% found that legislation favored them just 30% of the time.

The wealth gap has been worsening for the last 40 years. It is not surprising that when you put wealthy individuals in charge of the laws, taxation, and spending that the wealthy do very well at the expense of the rest of us. Citizens Congress could reverse this trend. If we put the full spectrum of Americans in Congress, we could expect to see significant changes. The top 1% of the wealthiest individuals would have about 1% of the seats in Congress, as they deserve. The same goes for the top 10% and the middle and lowest earners. We have the principle of one person/one vote. When wealthy individuals and corporations can buy the legislation they want, the one person/one vote principle does not go very far. We believe a Congress of Citizens is the surest path to an equitable society. Congress is broken, but we can fix it.

BY OCCUPATION:

About 40% of Congressmen are lawyers. Lawyers do very well in our country, and rank among the highest paid professionals. It is not surprising that a Congress with so many lawyers would pass laws that favor lawyers. The remaining seats have many educators, a fair number of physicians, and many lifelong politicians. They are quite different overall from the American population as a whole. We need a greater cross section of American workers. Citizens Congress, by using random selection, would automatically give us a mix of professions and trades, and a mix of those self-employed in various sized business, as well as employees from blue to white collar.   A Citizens Congress would look like us.

"If our nation is to rebuild opportunity for future generations, it will require our elected leaders to realize that their responsibility lies not with their political party, but rather with the American people that they have been chosen to represent."

Ami Bera

BY PARTY AFFILIATION:

When election time rolls around all we hear about is the Republicans and Democrats. It is surprising to find that they are both minority parties by a wide margin. Only 24 percent of voters are Republican and 28 percent Democrat. Forty two percent of us register as independent, but have only two seats in Congress. That is forty two percent of the voters represented by 0.5% of Congressional seats. This is despite the fact that 12 states have completely closed primary systems and 21 states have mixed primary systems. That means that Citizens are restricted or prohibited from voting for the candidate of their choice, but must vote within their own party in the primary elections. Many voters register with a party just to retain the right to vote in the primaries. It is likely that the true number of independent voters is over 50%. With the system we have now, when one party has a majority in both houses, they wield 90% of the power in Congress while representing only about

24 to 28 percent of the voters. With a Citizens Congress, the 1000 members would always come within about 3 percentage points of representing the population as a whole. That is very different from the bitterly divided partisanship we endure now. Citizens Congress automatically remedies these injustices and gives every demographic their fair share of representatives in the House. Congress is broken, we can fix this.

WILL CITIZENS BE REQUIRED TO SERVE?

No one will be required to serve. Anyone selected may simply decline. The next person chosen as an alternate will be invited, until someone chooses to accept. For those who do choose to sit in Congress they will be among their peers. If someone is so unfit to serve that two thirds of the House votes them out, they will be replaced by their alternate. The 1000 that do serve their one year term in office will be an accurate sampling of the population as a whole. We will, finally, have the representative government we deserve.

"If we were left solely to the wordy wit of legislators in Congress for our guidance, uncorrected by the seasonal experience and the effectual complaints of the people, America would not long retain her rank among the nations."

Author: Henry David Thoreau

IS THE GENERAL PUBLIC QUALIFIED TO SERVE?

I defer again to Thomas Jefferson:

"I know of no safe repository for the ultimate powers of society but the people themselves; and if we think them not enlightened enough to exercise their control with a wholesome discretion, the remedy is not to take it from them, but to increase their discretion by education."

We have a diverse population. Not everyone is well educated or versed in government affairs. There will be a preparatory period to address that. Remember that these 1000 registered voters are the same people we trust to vote for who should represent them in local, state, and federal elections. It seems much harder to judge who will do a good job, than to just go and do the job yourself.

These are the same people we trust to sit on juries. They decide the guilt or innocence of the accused, and almost always get it right based on the evidence presented and letter of the law. Few of us would want to trade a jury of our peers for any other system.

We cannot be accurately represented by two parties or 100. Each of us holds a range of opinions. Few are totally on the left or right. We might be pro-choice and pro-gun rights. We might love the environment, but own a lot of oil stock. We vary in intelligence, temperament, and sentiment. However, the vast majority of us love our country and want every person to get a fair chance. We are the people who go to war to preserve freedom for our nation and for others. We are the people who go to work every day and keep the country moving. We are not perfect, but the vast majority of us are good, decent people, and can be counted on to do the right thing. We can be trusted.

We will not just be thrown into Congress on day one and told to make laws. We will sit in Congress for one year but the year before we serve will be a year of preparation.

The first year, while continuing our normal lives at home, we will receive Congressional briefings. We will take courses online or at a local school on American history, government, and the Constitution. We will be required to obtain a passing grade on those courses. They might be similar in difficulty to the tests taken by legal immigrants to obtain Citizenship. This is needed because serving in Congress is a job. There are qualifications as one might find in any employment. The job requires the ability to read and comprehend what we have read. It requires the ability to listen and comprehend. It is similar to a classroom situation. These minimal requirements are needed to insure that those that sit in the House are capable of fulfilling their task. They will be compensated for the time spent in the first year, and earn full time pay for the second.

We might also ask ourselves about the current Congress. Are they fit to serve? With a 16% approval rating it seems most of us do not think so.

Our Congress has put the wealthiest country in the world, trillions of dollars in debt, with no plan to pay it off.

Congress, likewise, has not fulfilled its duty to maintain the infrastructure in our country. It is their job to provide the funds to maintain the roads, bridges, dams, and waterways, at the Federal level. For example, while we rank second in highway infrastructure spending, we fall into 60th place for road safety. We are spending lots of money, but not getting good results. This also lies at the feet of Congress

Our Congress has the sole authority to declare war, but has not done so since World War II. Millions of our soldiers have been sent into battle since WWII. More than 100,000 have not come home.

Less than 20% of Congressmen have served in the military and far fewer in combat. We seldom see their own children sent into harm's way.

It seems they lack not only the willingness to serve, but even to do their sworn duty. They take an oath to uphold the Constitution, but do not have the courage to stand up and vote for the battles they send our children to fight. Since World War II Congress has abdicated its duty by allowing Presidents to order our troops into battle without a declaration of war. A Citizens Congress, not fearing reelection, could pass a resolution limiting the President's power to send troops to battle to 30 or 60 days. That is plenty of time for the People to decide if the cause is worthy.

It is painfully obvious that Congress is not doing a good job and 84% of you agree. Congress is broken and it is time for a common sense solution to fix it.

OTHER ISSUES

ALTERNATES:

Each state will, in addition to those chosen to serve in Congress, provide alternates. The alternates will be chosen by lottery in the same way as members. They will receive the same briefings and have the same educational requirements as members. They will receive the same compensation for their time during the preparatory year. If any member is unable to serve their full term the alternate will be ready to step in.

TYRANNY OF THE MINORITY:

Many political thinkers have voiced opinions about the "tyranny of the majority". It is the fear that a direct democracy might allow a majority to trample the rights of a minority. That fear is not totally unfounded. Many issues have a nearly equal number of supporters and detractors. If 501 members of a Citizens Congress pass a certain law, tax, or rule affecting our benefits it is likely that a significant minority will not approve of their decision.

We do have the courts and the constitution to prevent many abuses. The President also has veto power, and any legislation passing with a veto proof two thirds majority is likely to be very popular.

However, we have something far worse in effect now. It is the "tyranny of the minority". A party line vote by either Republicans or Democrats would represent the voices of only 24 to 28 percent of the people but be imposed on everyone. In December of 2017 a major tax bill was approved along party lines. Although about two thirds of the public disapproved of the bill, it still passed with almost all members of one party voting for it and no members of the other party approving it. Members representing about 24 percent of the voters were able to pass major legislation despite a vast majority of the public opposing it. We can stop partisan politics from having undue control of our government. A

Citizens Congress is the closest we can come to achieving a truly fair and representative government. No one can represent us better than us.

PRIMARY DUTIES OF THE THREE BRANCHES

LEGISLATIVE (CONGRESS)

• Passes bills and makes the laws at the federal level

• Controls taxes and spending

• Controls the Federal budget

• Has the power to borrow money on our credit

• Regulates inter-state commerce

•	Has the sole power to declare war

•	Makes rules for the government and its officers

•	Defines the law in cases not specified by the Constitution

•	Ratifies treaties

•	Raises and regulates the military.

•	Confirms the Presidential nomination of Supreme Court judges and other officials.

•	Has the power of impeachment and trial. Can remove federal executives and judicial officers from office

EXECUTIVE (PRESIDENT)·

Acts as commander-in-chief of the armed forces

•	Executes the laws passed by Congress.

- Exercises veto power, but may be overridden by a two thirds vote in both houses of Congress

- May declare states of emergency

- Issues executive orders

- May make executive agreements (without ratification)

- Signs treaties (ratification requires approval by two-thirds of the Senate)

- Makes appointments to the Federal judiciary and executive departments

- Has the power pardon for Federal offenses, except in cases of impeachment

JUDICIAL

(SUPREME COURT AND LOWER COURTS)

**•	Interprets the constitution and reviews the constitutionality of laws**

**•	Acts as the highest judicial body in the nation, the court of last resort**

These are tasks that affect the daily lives of every American. To allow any party that represents the wishes of barely a quarter of our Citizens to have so much control is very different from representative government. Citizens Congress can fix this serious flaw in our system by vesting most of the power of Congress in the hands of ordinary Citizens.

"Leaders who do not help the people must be replaced by the people."

DaShanne Stokes

THE PROBLEMS WITH THE CONGRESS WE HAVE

PARTISANSHIP:

For most of our history, politics was considered the art of compromise. Party members reached across the isles and tried to find common ground. Statesmen worked for the good of the country rather than their party. Even hard core politicians saw the wisdom of negotiation and compromise. Now we see extremists serving in both parties and it is crippling our ability to govern. We see government shutdowns over bruised egos. We see good legislation that cannot pass because of extreme pressure to vote along party lines. We hear moderates, on both sides, complain of the lack of cooperation and bullying by party leaders. Many Congressmen are dissatisfied. They came to Congress to serve their country only to find themselves hamstrung by the demand to vote along party lines or according to the wishes of their donors.

Today, the partisanship in politics has seeped out into our society. We have family members not speaking to each other over the candidate they voted for in the last election. There are those who fan the flames of partisanship, but whose cause is not patriotism or sincerely held beliefs but the desire for money and power. Divide and conquer is one of the oldest tactics known to man. Lincoln warned us of the fate of *"a house divided"*.

All of this happens against a background where 42 percent of us would not claim membership in either party. By a good margin, independents are the largest bloc of voters, but have only two Senators and not one seat in the House of Representatives. That is, 42 percent of the voters, who have less than one-half of one percent representation. How can this be considered representative government?

CHECKS AND BALANCES:

The founders worked diligently on the Constitution to insure the rights of individual, protect the rights of the states, and establish a Federal government strong enough to endure. Toward those ends, they created three branches of government. These were the **Executive**, **Legislative**, and the **Judicial**. They were intended to be co-equal branches and act to check and balance each other's powers.

Congress could pass laws, but the President could veto those laws. The President could veto, but Congress could override with a two-thirds majority. A bill that became law was subject to review by the Supreme Court who bore the responsibility of determining its constitutionality. A President could issue an executive order but the Supreme Court could rule on whether he had exceeded his authority. The Supreme Court could rule something unconstitutional, but Congress could send a Constitutional

Amendment to the states for ratification. It was a well thought out system. The political parties however prevent this system from functioning as it should.

When one party holds both houses at the same time, they wind up with 90% of the political power of Congress. Both parties however are minority parties. The Republican Party represents about 24% of voters, and the Democrats about 28%. How can we allow such a concentration of power and still consider ourselves a democracy? When the President is of the same party as both houses, then that party has 95% of the power of two branches vested in one minority party. If this situation lasts very long, that same minority party can load up the Supreme Court with members of the same ideology, producing a lock on political power.

The other party is shut out, as well as the 42% of constituents who are registered independents. It is easy to have a large majority of voters with no political power for years at a time. Their needs and desires are largely ignored. If your party happens to currently be in power, do not get too comfortable. America has a long history of throwing out the presiding party and giving the other side a chance to rule.

When power is split, we see gridlock. A President from party A can do little when working with both Houses of Congress from party B. When the House of Representatives and the Senate are from different parties they do not work well with each other. No one wants to allow a law to be passed that makes the other party look good. We have seen party A vote against legislation proposed by party B, even when it was originally the idea of party A.

When one party is in control, we see bad legislation passed that few Americans approve of. When power is split, we see good legislation that does not become law because of partisan politics.

The People however are not nearly as partisan as the political world. Few of us are die-hard members of our party. At least 42% of us claim no party affiliation at all. Independents are the largest largest bloc of voters. In addition to that, the 42% only have 2 members in Congress. That is because the 2 largest political parties have a death grip on the election process. We are one nation. We are one people. We are diverse. We are much more diverse than two, or ten parties could represent. The only people who can clearly, fairly, equitability, represent US is US. Just as we sit in the jury box, listen carefully, deliberate thoughtfully, and almost always come to a fair decision, we can sit in Congress and represent our country. Citizens Congress is the only plan that allows a truly representative government. WE THE PEOPLE, can have it if we want it. Congress is broken and we can fix it.

WHAT ABOUT THE PRESIDENCY?

There is no change in our amendment to the office of the President. The President retains veto power. Congress retains the ability to overrule the veto with a two thirds majority vote. Citizens Congress however would have an important, positive impact on the Presidency. Currently, a President without a Congress of his party has a nearly impossible task of getting laws passed. This is true, even if they are great laws that would benefit the country. Congress has become so partisan that any success by a President is seen as a defeat to the opposing party. On the other hand, a bad idea from a President who had majorities in both houses might get rubber stamped by his own party, and become law even against the wishes of the great majority of voters. Citizens Congress corrects this. If a President presents a good idea to a

Citizens Congress every member would be free to vote his conscience regardless of party affiliation or lack of affiliation. Likewise bad proposals would not stand a chance. Good leaders would be enhanced and poor leaders' mistakes would be minimized. The effects of Congress are far reaching. Not only would we have a better Congress, but we would have a better Presidency. The Supreme Court likewise would be enhanced. Currently, each party tries to load the court with judges as far left, or right as they can hope to get approved. The parties are fighting for ideologies that are further to the extremes than that of most Americans. A Citizens Congress would tend to approve of only the most qualified, and likely, the more moderate of those nominated. Citizens Congress will not provide us with a perfect government. It will provide us with a much better government than we have now. It is worth working for.

FUNDRAISING:

Representatives presently serve two-year terms. It is well established that they spend twenty or more hours a week calling donors asking for campaign donations. This, plus the time they spend campaigning, means we are paying for full time employees and getting part time work. In addition, the donors they are calling are not people who send $5.00 donations. They are soliciting money from wealthy individuals and corporations all of whom want some return on their investment. At the very least, the donors are watching the voting records carefully. If they want to continue to receive money from an oil company, union, agricultural conglomerate, environmental group, or pharmaceutical company, they know how they have to vote. Citizens Congress takes the money out of elections by taking elections out of the House of Representatives and publicly funding Senate elections. It makes the House truly "Representative".

We are not stuck with the system we have. There is a way forward, but we must come together and work for it.

Plata o Plomo:

Silver or Lead:

It was Pablo Escobar that made the phrase "plata o plomo" infamous. It means literally "silver or lead". The drug kingpin would make this offer to government officials, the army, and police officers. It meant simply, take the bribe, or I will have you killed. It was a very effective negotiation technique. Our Congressmen face a less deadly version of the same offer. Lobbyists and party leaders can offer Congressmen millions in campaign funds to pass the desired legislation and vote along party lines. Now however, in addition to the carrot, they often add the stick. If you do not do as we demand, we will put another candidate up for election against you and fund them very well. It may not be as extreme as the drug cartels offer, but it is still thug behavior and has changed many votes. Citizens Congress can deprive the bad actors in our democracy from wielding this power over our representatives. We need Congressmen who are free to vote their conscience, and do what is best for their country and its people, not their party. Citizens Congress can give us that Congress.

LOBBYISTS:

The law that makes lobbyists possible is a very good law and does not need to be changed. It is the First Amendment to the Constitution that guarantees *"the right of the people peaceably to assemble, and to petition the Government for a redress of grievances"*.

I have walked the halls of Congress and entered into the offices of many Congressmen. It is quite an easy process. Across from the Capital building there are buildings that contain the offices of all the Representatives and Senators. After passing through security one may walk freely down the halls, and the names of the Congressmen and the States they represent are on their door. If you walk through one of those doors you will be in the office of the Congressman of your choice. A staff member will greet you and ask if they can assist you. Your chances of actually speaking with a

Congressman depend principally on one thing. What can you offer your representative? If you are a very wealthy individual or corporate donor, or a lobbyist representing the same, you will likely get a warm welcome. One can expect the same if they represent a large block of voters. That could be a trade union, environmental organization, or political movement for example. If you can offer money or votes your chances of having a meeting with the representative are good. Even an individual has the right to try. There is actually nothing wrong with a major oil company, for example, wanting some input into energy policy. Oil companies play a crucial role in keeping our country moving. The problems come in when the company is petitioning for their own self-interest with disregard to the impact on the public. If they are only concerned about their profit margins at the expense of the rest of us, we have cause for concern. Even those who are self-serving though still have the right to be so. The problem comes in when they can walk in with a check for $200,000.00 in one hand and the legislation they hope will benefit their business in the other. This form of open bribery is now completely legal. The Citizens Congress amendment would eliminate this corruption of our political system. They could still "*petition their Government*" but only with their ideas, not their money.

Without infringing upon the right to petition the Government, we could also insist that any person petitioning Congress that represents anyone other than himself (lobbyist for a corporation, union, etc.) must submit their proposals in a public forum (by e-mail for example) to put an end to backroom deals made out of the public eye.

Based on information from the Senate Office of Public Records the Center for Responsive Politics estimates that over 12,000 lobbyists spend $3 billion dollars a year lobbying Congress. That's over $3 million per congressman. Some of this comes from environmentalists and unions, but most it from wealthy individuals and large corporations. When businessmen spend money they expect a return on investment. If a million spent on lobbying yields $100 million in tax breaks, reduced regulations, or government contracts, that is an excellent return on investment. More often than not, I suspect those votes, which are bought and paid for, are not in the best interest of the average American. We have many cases where lobbyists have actually written the legislation they wanted, handed it to their congressional representative, and seen it passed into law. A popular joke is *"a certain corporation had such a bad year they had to lay off three Congressmen"*. It is a cute joke but too close to the truth to be funny for the rest of us. A Citizens Congress could ban the type of lobbying we currently have and say "if we want your opinion we will ask for it." Then if an issue came up, on energy production for example, they could invite the industries involved along with scientists, environmental experts, and other interested parties to testify before Congress under oath. Those who choose to lie or present false data would face prison time for perjury. Citizens Congress fixes the problem of undue influence by banning lobbyist's money from the House of Representatives and the Senate.

A HOUSE DIVIDED

It was Abraham Lincoln that warned us of the fate of *"a house divided"*. Partisan politics was once largely limited to election time. Politicians would say horrible things about each other, both true and untrue, and then when elected work fairly well together. As politics turned from a *"Gentleman's game"* to a *"blood sport"* the bitterness increased, and working together as statesmen united for the good of the country became difficult to impossible. This was bad enough, but it was still just politics and politics is the price we pay for democracy.

This is not to say that all Congressmen are corrupt. There are many who are sickened by the bitter divineness in today's political arena. Record numbers of members are leaving Congress. Many complain of being bullied to vote along party lines or to please large donors. Citizens Congress can expect support from those members willing to put country, and the love and respect they have for their fellow Citizens, above party loyalty or even self-interest.

Now however partisanship has spilled over into the public arena. More and more Americans are divided against each other. People repost horrible lies about the politicians they hate on Facebook. Family member are no longer speaking to each other, based on whom they voted for in the last election. The power brokers of this country love it. They want to see working people vote against their own self-interests while fighting with words, and sometime clubs and guns, against their neighbors. The last thing they want to see is the American middle class, the working people, and the working poor, who make everything happen in this country, come together in unity and demand a fair deal.

We stand on the brink of oligarchy, where the very rich have most of the political power and We the People are the only ones who can end that. We can do it by passing the Citizens Congress Amendment, which will shift the balance of power solidly to the large majority of hard working decent people who are the heart and soul of our country. I am not asking you to believe in me. I am telling you that I believe in you. I trust that if you sit in Congress and feel the weight of responsibility settle on your shoulders that you will listen carefully, examine the evidence, vote your conscience, and do the right thing. It will not create a perfect government. Each of us will find ourselves disagreeing some of the time with your decisions. But, we the people will have the government envisioned over two hundred years ago. We will fulfill the dream of Abraham Lincoln that we *"shall have a new birth of freedom-and that* **government of the people, by the people, for the people shall not perish from the earth."**

Dan Barnett,

Founder of Citizens Congress Inc.

December 31st, 2017

Revised September 26, 2018

"The art and science of asking questions is the source of all knowledge"

Thomas Berger

FREQUENTLY ASKED QUESTIONS

How will Representatives be chosen?

They will be chosen by lottery. A formal name for this is sortition. It is a process which insures that all American Citizens who are registered to vote have an equal opportunity to serve. It will be up to each state to choose their representatives by a process proven unprejudiced and truly random.

Who does the choosing?

Each state will be responsible for administration of their lottery system to insure it is truly random and inclusive.

Who is eligible?

Any United States citizen who is a registered voter.

Are there any other requirements?

Serving in Congress is a job. Like any job, there are prerequisites to insure that the applicant is capable of preforming then needed tasks. To serve well in Congress, one must be able to absorb new information, and make decisions based on that information. It is a similar process to classroom learning and testing. Each person chosen to be a Representative or alternate would be given classes in American history, government, and the Constitution. A passing score would be required. The degree of difficulty might be similar to the Citizenship test required of new citizens.

Would there be any other preparation required?

Each member and alternate would receive regular Security Briefings and Congressional Briefings during the preparatory year on National Security and issues before Congress.

What about people who are blind, or deaf?

The Americans with Disabilities Act (ADA) will be followed to insure no discrimination against any person with limited abilities.

Is service mandatory, like the draft?

No. Service is voluntary.

How long would they serve?

Members would sit in Congress for one year. In the year prior to service, they would receive training and updates about issues before Congress as well as National Security briefings.

Would there be educational requirements?

Only the ability to pass the courses given during the preparatory year would be required. My mother had a 9th grade education, yet maintained a balanced budget while raising three kids alone, and retired comfortably. I have friends with degrees who are retirement age and broke. Our very well educated Congress has only given us a balanced budget for four years since 1970. We have not been debt free since Andrew Jackson was President. A randomly selected Congress would represent the full spectrum of intellectual abilities (subject to only by the above-mentioned capacity to demonstrate learning ability through course work).

Can we trust those 18 to 24 years old to make important decisions and shoulder such responsibility?

 We already do. The vast majority of those who serve in combat on the front lines are in that age group. They may make life and death decisions and have the greatest burden of responsibility of citizenship. They deserve a voice in Congress.

How does Citizens Congress affect women?

Women make up about 51% of voters, but hold only 19% of the seats in Congress. A Citizens Congress would insure the House would have women in about half of the seats.

How are political parties affected?

The parties have far too much power now. Only 28% of voters are Democratic, and 24% are Republican. Yet when one of these parties holds both houses, they wield 90% of the power in Congress. The 42% of us who are registered independents hold only 2 seats in Congress. Not 2%, just two seats. That is 0.5% for the largest group of voters.

Why are we messing with the Constitution? The Founding Fathers knew what they were doing when they wrote it.

That was not the opinion of the Founders. When Benjamin Franklin made the last argument for ratification before the final vote, many were still opposed. Franklin did not argue that the Constitution was the perfect document for all time. He pointed out that many things he believed in his youth, were now repugnant to him, and that many things he embraced now, he once hated. He argued that the Constitution was not perfect, but good enough. It was expected that the document would change over time. The Founders included the Amendment process for that purpose. The vote passed on a document considered to be "good enough". It was only two years later when we ratified the first ten amendments, The Bill of Rights.

Thomas Jefferson once offered the opinion that we might need a new constitution ever twenty years because; one generation should not be bound by the thinking of the previous generation. He opined that *the earth belongs to the living" and the dead have neither powers nor rights.*" We honor the Founders for their courage in fighting the war, their vision in bring forth a new form of government, and for their humility in allowing a process by which their preeminent document could be transformed by future generations.

Why should the Senate vote to limit their own power?

Many Senators are frustrated with the pressure to vote along party lines. They also need to spend endless hours on the telephone begging wealthy donors for money and engaging with lobbyists. Citizens Congress would allow Senators to regain their independence, and dignity. They would be free to vote their conscience. Any Senator or group of Senators could send proposals to the House. There the people would decide, on merit, not partisanship. Old school politicians and the corrupt who love back room deals might squeal, but statesmen with integrity would thrive with their new independence. There would be more opportunity to bring forth new ideas, and to demonstrate leadership and statesmanship.

There are many who sit in Congress now who are sickened by what Congress has become. They hate spending so much time begging for money. They hate being forced to vote for legislation they do not believe in by pressure from party leaders, or donors looking over their shoulders.

There are members of Congress who are already willing to vote for a Citizens Congress. There are people who are willing to lose their jobs to retain their integrity.

The Citizens Congress organization, and their supporters, would ask persons running for the U.S. Congress and for their state legislature to pledge to vote in favor of the Amendment as a condition of their re-election. Citizens could put enough pressure on our state and federal legislators to insure their vote for Citizens Congress. However, we must want it and we must work for it. It is not easy, but it is possible if we work together.

Do you really think this is possible?

We are living in a time when many things that once seemed impossible, are taken for granted. Indeed many former impossible things seem as though they were actually inevitable.

In America there was an abolishment movement for at least 100 years before slavery ended. Generations of slaves and abolitionists lived their whole lives without seeing any progress at all toward the goal of freedom. Then one day, the shackles came off. It seems inevitable now that slavery had to end.

Before 1776 virtually the entire world was ruled by tyrants, by one name or another, and had been for most of human history. Democracy seemed to be an impossible fantasy. Freedom for Citizens to choose their own leaders was a pipe dream for those who even dared to dream it. From that first bold step in 1776 we have seen the number of democracies grow to 123 in a little over two hundred and forty years. Countries not considered democracies number just 72. Dictatorships are doomed. Their time is coming to an end, just as surely as widespread slavery and torture are no longer ideas that can be sustained.

I believe, that in less than 100 years, every country on our planet will be a democracy and will use random selection to choose their legislative bodies. It is not impossible. It is, I believe, inevitable.

"Freedom lies in being bold"

Robert Frost

PROPOSED 28TH AMENDMENT TO THE CONSTITUTION OF THE UNITED STATES OF AMERICA

This is a first draft. It will be subject to review by constitutional scholars and attorneys, as well as the general public. As with the Constitution, it will be carefully reviewed and edited to insure its intention is clear and to avoid unintended consequences. The final document will reflect the best thinking of many minds. This draft does however thoughtfully represent the spirit of self-

governance the author hopes will be entrusted to
the American people.

28th Amendment to the Constitution of the United States of America

First Draft

All legislative Powers herein granted shall be vested in a Congress of the United States, which shall consist of a Senate and House of Representatives.

The House of Representatives shall be composed of Members chosen each Year by lottery from the pool of registered voters of the several States. Further qualifications of those selected shall be that they shall, during the year prior to their service, attend such classes as shall be deemed fit, and obtain a passing grade in those classes. This requirement is necessary to insure a level of competency for the job of serving in the House of Representatives. Alternates shall be chosen in the same fashion to assume the duties in the event the original representative is unable to complete their term of office. The number of representatives shall be 1000 selected from an equal number of districts apportioned among the states according to their population.

No Person shall be a Representative who shall not have attained to the age of eighteen years, and been seven years a Citizen of the United States, and who shall not, when selected, be an inhabitant of that State and district in which he shall be chosen.

The Senate shall consist of two Senators from each state chosen by the voters of each state.

The Senate shall be divided as equally as may be into three Classes. The Seats of the Senators of the first Class shall be vacated at the Expiration of the second year, of the second Class at the Expiration of the fourth year, and of the third Class at the Expiration of the sixth year, so that one third may be chosen every second year; and if Vacancies happen by Resignation, or otherwise, during the Recess of the Legislature of any State, the Executive thereof may make temporary Appointments until the next Meeting of the Legislature, which shall then fill such Vacancies.

No Person shall be a Senator who shall not have attained to the age of thirty years, and been nine years a Citizen of the United States, and who shall not, when elected, be an Inhabitant of that State for which he shall be chosen.

The Vice President of the United States shall be President of the Senate, but shall have no Vote, unless they be equally divided.

The Senate shall choose their other Officers, and also a President pro tempore, in the Absence of the Vice President, or when he shall exercise the Office of President of the United States.

The House of Representatives shall have the sole Power to try all Impeachments. When sitting for that Purpose, they shall be on Oath or Affirmation. When the President of the United States is tried, the Chief Justice shall preside: And no Person shall be convicted without the Concurrence of two thirds of the Members present.

Judgment in Cases of Impeachment shall not extend further than to removal from Office, and disqualification to hold and enjoy any Office of honor, Trust or Profit under the United States: but the Party convicted shall nevertheless be liable and subject to Indictment, Trial, Judgment and Punishment, according to Law.

The Times, Places and Manner of holding Elections for Senators shall be prescribed in each State by the Legislature thereof; but the Congress may at any time by Law make or alter such Regulations, except as to the Places of choosing Senators.

The Congress shall assemble at least once in every year, and such Meeting shall be on the Second Monday in January, unless they shall by Law appoint a different Day.

Section 5

Each House shall be the Judge of the Elections, Returns and Qualifications of its own Members, and a Majority of each shall constitute a Quorum to do Business; but a smaller Number may adjourn from day to day, and may be authorized to compel the Attendance of absent Members, in such Manner, and under such Penalties as each House may provide.

Each House may determine the Rules of its Proceedings, punish its Members for disorderly Behavior, and, with the Concurrence of two thirds, expel a Member.

Each House shall keep a Journal of its Proceedings, and from time to time publish the same, excepting such Parts as may in their Judgment require Secrecy; and the Yeas and Nays of the Members of either House on any question shall, at the Desire of one fifth of those Present, be entered on the Journal.

The Senate shall propose and pass such legislation and resolutions as they see fit according to the rules of the Senate. Such legislation and resolutions shall be passed to the House of Representatives for approval.

The House of Representatives may approve, reject, or amend, any legislation or resolutions by majority vote. The House may likewise propose and pass any legislation and resolutions they see fit. Such legislation shall be sent to the Senate for comment, but shall not require approval by the Senate. If approved by a majority vote in the House, such legislation and resolutions shall be sent to the President for his signature or veto. If the President signs such legislation, it will become law. If the President does not sign such legislation within ten calendar days, it shall become law without his signature. If the President shall veto such legislation, it shall be returned to the House of Representatives for further consideration. If the House shall vote by two thirds to overturn the President's veto, it shall become law.

CITIZENS CONGRESS INC.

The author is Founder and President of Citizens Congress Inc.. It is registered in the state of Florida as a non-profit organization and with the IRS with a 501 c4 status.

Citizens Congress Inc. is a non-partisan organization with one purpose. We exist to propose, promote, and ultimately help pass, a Constitutional Amendment to bring true democracy to America. We believe Congress is broken, and there is a way to fix it.

We submit that ordinary Citizens, chosen by a random lottery system, can best represent the interests and needs of the American public.

Our position on every issue is,

"Put the People in Power, and Let the People Decide."

We hope the information in this book will encourage you to support the idea of Citizen Governance and Representative Democracy.

If you would like to help, here are some things you can do:

Talk to your friends, relatives, neighbors, and co-workers. The idea of true self-government needs to discussed and brought to the front of our political conversation.

Go to Citizens Congress Inc. on Facebook. Like us, Follow us, and share the messages.

Go to our webpage:

www.citizenscongressinc.org

and chose the **SUPPORT US** page. Sign up as a supporter. When we go to Congress or our state legislators, we need the power of numbers. We need to show that we are representing millions of voters who are demanding better government. We can only do that with your support.

Make a donation:

Donating is easy.

Online, go to our website www.citizenscongressinc.org

And click the DONATE button.

If you prefer to donate by mail, please send your check made out to **Citizens Congress Inc.** to

Citizens Congress Inc.

P O BOX 1691

Lake Worth, FL 33461-1691

Your support is the most important thing, yet every organization needs money to operate. As of this date (September 26, 2018) all of our operating expenses are funded privately. Every dollar you donate is used to present this information to more people. We can get our message in front of the public for as little as a penny per person, per view. We spend your money carefully. Our finances are completely transparent, and our books are open to everyone. We know you need to trust those you give to, and we intend to always be worthy of that trust.

CONTACT INFORMATION

If you would like more information, please see:

www.citizenscongressinc.org

At the **citizenscongressinc.org** website, you will be able to obtain the latest news about our organization, and what is currently happening in Congress. You will also be able to sign up as a supporter, and if you wish, a donor.

To reach the author, send email to

dan@citizenscongressinc.org

ABOUT THE AUTHOR

Dan Barnett is the founder of Citizens Congress Incorporated, a non-partisan, grassroots, Not for Profit Corporation dedicated to the writing, promotion, and passage of a Constitutional Amendment to change the structure of the U.S. Congress. The extreme partisanship of our political system has led him to believe that we need the full spectrum of American citizens to represent us in Congress, rather than the professional politicians we currently have.

Two themes dominated his life. Fixing things that were broken, and communications. From childhood, he was always repairing things around the house. Friends call him "MacGyver" for his ever present Swiss Army Knife and handy skills. Congress is the most broken thing in our country and Dan wants to help fix it.

In the Navy, from 1969 to 1973, he was in communications and then worked for AT&T as a communications technician. Becoming a photographer, writer, and speaker came later in life.

Dan is a lifelong learner interested in history and the sciences. He has travelled to every state and more than 60 countries. His most important qualification is a lifetime as an average American citizen. Spending half of his working life as a small business owner, and the rest employed by large corporations, he understands the problems of working people and their nobility.

Dan was born on a farm in Tennessee and picked cotton as a child on the family plot. By the time he reached High School he had moved to the city and embraced urban life and thinking. He is a bridge between two worlds. He has friends and family across the entire political spectrum, and understands they are all good decent people. He knows that partisan politics weakens our nation and that working together will strengthen it.

He has four children and two grandchildren. Like all of you, he wants to pass on to them a better world.

He is dedicated to the cause of Citizen Government and has faith that the American people, when given the responsibility of governance, will do the right thing.

EPILOGUE

Thank you for taking the time to read Citizens Congress. I have undertaken to inspire the people of America with new hope for a better government, a better life, and a better world. The Athenians of Ancient Greece chose their legislative body and many other government positions by lottery for over 180 years. It was their belief that elected representation would inevitably lead to oligarchy. During that time, they made their mark on the world in the sciences, mathematic, the arts, and philosophy.

Citizens Congress is an old idea brought back to life. It is from Proverbs that we are told *"Where this is no vision, the people perish."*

It is my hope that millions of Citizens will rise up and do the work needed, to bring this vision of truly representative government into the world.

America is a great country. We brought democracy into the modern world, and many gave their lives to preserve it here and around the globe.

Our greatest days do not have to be behind us. We can forge a future better than our past, if we have the courage, and the will, to live up to our highest ideals.

Thank you, Dan Barnett

Notes:

Notes:

Notes: